This Planner Belongs To :

_____

Printed by CreateSpace, An Amazon.com Company
A Publication by Jada Correia

Success Doesn't Just Happen It's Planned For.

Monthly Budget

Income		
Income 1		
Income 2		
Other Income		
TOTAL INCOME		

Expenses

Month :

Budget :

Bill To Be Paid	Date Due	Amount	Paid	Note
			◯	
			◯	
			◯	
			◯	
			◯	
			◯	
			◯	
			◯	
			◯	
			◯	
			◯	
			◯	
			◯	
			◯	
			◯	
			◯	
			◯	
			◯	
			◯	
TOTAL				

Monthly Budget

Other Expenses	Date	Amount	Note
TOTAL			

TOTAL INCOME

TOTAL EXPENSES

DIFFERENCE

Notes

Weekly Expense Tracker

Month :   **Week Of :**   **Budget :**

Monday   Date ..../......./.......

Description	Amount
Total	

Tuesday   Date ..../......./.......

Description	Amount
Total	

Wednesday   Date ..../......./.......

Description	Amount
Total	

Thursday   Date ..../......./.......

Description	Amount
Total	

Weekly Expense Tracker

Total Expenses :   Balance :

Friday   Date ....../....../......

Description	Amount
Total	

Saturday   Date ....../....../......

Description	Amount
Total	

Sunday   Date ....../....../......

Description	Amount
Total	

Notes

Weekly Expense Tracker

Month :   Week Of :   Budget :

Monday   Date ....../....../......

Description	Amount
Total	

Tuesday   Date ....../....../......

Description	Amount
Total	

Wednesday   Date ....../....../......

Description	Amount
Total	

Thursday   Date ....../....../......

Description	Amount
Total	

Weekly Expense Tracker

Total Expenses :   **Balance :**

Friday   Date ..../......../........

Description	Amount
Total	

Saturday   Date ..../......../........

Description	Amount
Total	

Sunday   Date ..../......../........

Description	Amount
Total	

Notes

Weekly Expense Tracker

Month : _____   Week Of : _____   Budget : _____

Monday   Date ..../......./.......

Description	Amount
Total	

Tuesday   Date ..../......./.......

Description	Amount
Total	

Wednesday   Date ..../......./.......

Description	Amount
Total	

Thursday   Date ..../......./.......

Description	Amount
Total	

Weekly Expense Tracker

Total Expenses : **Balance :**

Friday
Date ....../....../......

Description	Amount
Total	

Saturday
Date ....../....../......

Description	Amount
Total	

Sunday
Date ....../....../......

Description	Amount
Total	

Notes

_____
_____
_____
_____
_____
_____
_____
_____
_____

Weekly Expense Tracker

Month : **Week Of :** **Budget :**

Monday
Date ….../….../…...

Description	Amount
Total	

Tuesday
Date ….../….../…...

Description	Amount
Total	

Wednesday
Date ….../….../…...

Description	Amount
Total	

Thursday
Date ….../….../…...

Description	Amount
Total	

Weekly Expense Tracker

Total Expenses :   **Balance :**

Friday   Date ..../......./.......

Description	Amount
Total	

Saturday   Date ..../......./.......

Description	Amount
Total	

Sunday   Date ..../......./.......

Description	Amount
Total	

Notes

Weekly Expense Tracker

Month :   Week Of :   Budget :

Monday   Date ….../….../…....

Description	Amount
Total	

Tuesday   Date ….../….../…....

Description	Amount
Total	

Wednesday   Date ….../….../…....

Description	Amount
Total	

Thursday   Date ….../….../…....

Description	Amount
Total	

Weekly Expense Tracker

Total Expenses :   **Balance :**

Friday   Date …...../…...../…......

Description	Amount
Total	

Saturday   Date …...../…...../…......

Description	Amount
Total	

Sunday   Date …...../…...../…......

Description	Amount
Total	

Notes

Monthly Budget

Income		
Income 1		
Income 2		
Other Income		
TOTAL INCOME		

Expenses

Month :

Budget :

Bill To Be Paid	Date Due	Amount	Paid	Note
			○	
			○	
			○	
			○	
			○	
			○	
			○	
			○	
			○	
			○	
			○	
			○	
			○	
			○	
			○	
			○	
			○	
			○	
			○	
TOTAL				

Monthly Budget

Other Expenses	Date	Amount	Note
TOTAL			

TOTAL INCOME

TOTAL EXPENSES

DIFFERENCE

Notes

Weekly Expense Tracker

Month : _____   Week Of : _____   Budget : _____

Monday
Date ..../......./.......

Description	Amount
Total	

Tuesday
Date ..../......./.......

Description	Amount
Total	

Wednesday
Date ..../......./.......

Description	Amount
Total	

Thursday
Date ..../......./.......

Description	Amount
Total	

Weekly Expense Tracker

Total Expenses : _____   Balance : _____

Friday   Date ....../....../......

Description	Amount
Total	

Saturday   Date ....../....../......

Description	Amount
Total	

Sunday   Date ....../....../......

Description	Amount
Total	

Notes

_____
_____
_____
_____
_____
_____
_____
_____
_____
_____

Weekly Expense Tracker

Month :   Week Of :   Budget :

Monday   Date ....../....../......

Description	Amount
Total	

Tuesday   Date ....../....../......

Description	Amount
Total	

Wednesday   Date ....../....../......

Description	Amount
Total	

Thursday   Date ....../....../......

Description	Amount
Total	

Weekly Expense Tracker

Total Expenses :   **Balance :**

Friday

Date ..../......./.......

Description	Amount
Total	

Saturday

Date ..../......./.......

Description	Amount
Total	

Sunday

Date ..../......./.......

Description	Amount
Total	

Notes

Weekly Expense Tracker

Month : _____   Week Of : _____   Budget : _____

Monday   Date ..../......./.......

Description	Amount
Total	

Tuesday   Date ..../......./.......

Description	Amount
Total	

Wednesday   Date ..../......./.......

Description	Amount
Total	

Thursday   Date ..../......./.......

Description	Amount
Total	

Weekly Expense Tracker

Total Expenses :   Balance :

Friday   Date ..../......./......

Description	Amount
Total	

Saturday   Date ..../......./......

Description	Amount
Total	

Sunday   Date ..../......./......

Description	Amount
Total	

Notes

_____
_____
_____
_____
_____
_____
_____
_____
_____
_____

Weekly Expense Tracker

Month : _____   Week Of : _____   Budget : _____

Monday   Date ..../......./.......

Description	Amount
Total	

Tuesday   Date ..../......./.......

Description	Amount
Total	

Wednesday   Date ..../......./.......

Description	Amount
Total	

Thursday   Date ..../......./.......

Description	Amount
Total	

Weekly Expense Tracker

Total Expenses :   **Balance :**

Friday   Date ....../....../......

Description	Amount
Total	

Saturday   Date ....../....../......

Description	Amount
Total	

Sunday   Date ....../....../......

Description	Amount
Total	

Notes

_____
_____
_____
_____
_____
_____
_____
_____
_____

Weekly Expense Tracker

Month : _____   Week Of : _____   Budget : _____

Monday   Date ..../......./.......

Description	Amount
Total	

Tuesday   Date ..../......./.......

Description	Amount
Total	

Wednesday   Date ..../......./.......

Description	Amount
Total	

Thursday   Date ..../......./.......

Description	Amount
Total	

Weekly Expense Tracker

Total Expenses :   **Balance :**

Friday   Date ..../......./.......

Description	Amount
Total	

Saturday   Date ..../......./.......

Description	Amount
Total	

Sunday   Date ..../......./.......

Description	Amount
Total	

Notes

_____
_____
_____
_____
_____
_____
_____
_____
_____
_____

Monthly Budget

Income		
Income 1		
Income 2		
Other Income		
TOTAL INCOME		

Expenses

Month :

Budget :

Bill To Be Paid	Date Due	Amount	Paid	Note
			○	
			○	
			○	
			○	
			○	
			○	
			○	
			○	
			○	
			○	
			○	
			○	
			○	
			○	
			○	
			○	
			○	
			○	
			○	
			○	
TOTAL				

Monthly Budget

Other Expenses	Date	Amount	Note
TOTAL			

TOTAL INCOME

TOTAL EXPENSES

DIFFERENCE

Notes

Weekly Expense Tracker

Month :   Week Of :   Budget :

Monday   Date ..../......./.......

Description	Amount
Total	

Tuesday   Date ..../......./.......

Description	Amount
Total	

Wednesday   Date ..../......./.......

Description	Amount
Total	

Thursday   Date ..../......./.......

Description	Amount
Total	

Weekly Expense Tracker

Total Expenses :   **Balance :**

Friday
Date ..../......./.......

Description	Amount
Total	

Saturday
Date ..../......./.......

Description	Amount
Total	

Sunday
Date ..../......./.......

Description	Amount
Total	

Notes

Weekly Expense Tracker

Month : _____   Week Of : _____   Budget : _____

Monday

Date ..../......../........

Description	Amount
Total	

Tuesday

Date ..../......../........

Description	Amount
Total	

Wednesday

Date ..../......../........

Description	Amount
Total	

Thursday

Date ..../......../........

Description	Amount
Total	

Weekly Expense Tracker

Total Expenses :   **Balance :**

Friday
Date ..../......./.......

Description	Amount
Total	

Saturday
Date ..../......./.......

Description	Amount
Total	

Sunday
Date ..../......./.......

Description	Amount
Total	

Notes

Weekly Expense Tracker

Month : _____   Week Of : _____   Budget : _____

Monday   Date ..../......./.......

Description	Amount
Total	

Tuesday   Date ..../......./.......

Description	Amount
Total	

Wednesday   Date ..../......./.......

Description	Amount
Total	

Thursday   Date ..../......./.......

Description	Amount
Total	

Weekly Expense Tracker

Total Expenses :   **Balance :**

Friday   Date ..../......./.......

Description	Amount
Total	

Saturday   Date ..../......./.......

Description	Amount
Total	

Sunday   Date ..../......./.......

Description	Amount
Total	

Notes

_____
_____
_____
_____
_____
_____
_____
_____
_____

Weekly Expense Tracker

Month :   **Week Of :**   **Budget :**

Monday
Date ..../......./.......

Description	Amount
Total	

Tuesday
Date ..../......./.......

Description	Amount
Total	

Wednesday
Date ..../......./.......

Description	Amount
Total	

Thursday
Date ..../......./.......

Description	Amount
Total	

Weekly Expense Tracker

Total Expenses :   Balance :

Friday   Date ..../......./.......

Description	Amount
Total	

Saturday   Date ..../......./.......

Description	Amount
Total	

Sunday   Date ..../......./.......

Description	Amount
Total	

Notes

Weekly Expense Tracker

Month :   Week Of :   Budget :

Monday   Date ..../......./.......

Description	Amount
Total	

Tuesday   Date ..../......./.......

Description	Amount
Total	

Wednesday   Date ..../......./.......

Description	Amount
Total	

Thursday   Date ..../......./.......

Description	Amount
Total	

Weekly Expense Tracker

Total Expenses :   **Balance :**

Friday   Date ..../......./.......

Description	Amount
Total	

Saturday   Date ..../......./.......

Description	Amount
Total	

Sunday   Date ..../......./.......

Description	Amount
Total	

Notes

Monthly Budget

Income		
Income 1		
Income 2		
Other Income		
TOTAL INCOME		

Expenses

Month :

Budget :

Bill To Be Paid	Date Due	Amount	Paid	Note
			○	
			○	
			○	
			○	
			○	
			○	
			○	
			○	
			○	
			○	
			○	
			○	
			○	
			○	
			○	
			○	
			○	
			○	
			○	
			○	
TOTAL				

Monthly Budget

Other Expenses	Date	Amount	Note
TOTAL			

TOTAL INCOME

TOTAL EXPENSES

DIFFERENCE

Notes

Weekly Expense Tracker

Month : _____   Week Of : _____   Budget : _____

Monday   Date ....../....../......

Description	Amount
Total	

Tuesday   Date ....../....../......

Description	Amount
Total	

Wednesday   Date ....../....../......

Description	Amount
Total	

Thursday   Date ....../....../......

Description	Amount
Total	

Weekly Expense Tracker

Total Expenses :   **Balance :**

Friday   Date ..../......./.......

Description	Amount
Total	

Saturday   Date ..../......./.......

Description	Amount
Total	

Sunday   Date ..../......./.......

Description	Amount
Total	

Notes

_____

_____

_____

_____

_____

_____

_____

_____

_____

Weekly Expense Tracker

Month :   Week Of :   Budget :

Monday   Date ..../......./.......

Description	Amount
Total	

Tuesday   Date ..../......./.......

Description	Amount
Total	

Wednesday   Date ..../......./.......

Description	Amount
Total	

Thursday   Date ..../......./.......

Description	Amount
Total	

Weekly Expense Tracker

Total Expenses :   Balance :

Friday   Date ..../......./.......

Description	Amount
Total	

Saturday   Date ..../......./.......

Description	Amount
Total	

Sunday   Date ..../......./.......

Description	Amount
Total	

Notes

Weekly Expense Tracker

Month : _____   Week Of : _____   Budget : _____

Monday   Date ..../......./.......

Description	Amount
Total	

Tuesday   Date ..../......./.......

Description	Amount
Total	

Wednesday   Date ..../......./.......

Description	Amount
Total	

Thursday   Date ..../......./.......

Description	Amount
Total	

Weekly Expense Tracker

Total Expenses :   Balance :

Friday   Date ....../....../......

Description	Amount
Total	

Saturday   Date ....../....../......

Description	Amount
Total	

Sunday   Date ....../....../......

Description	Amount
Total	

Notes

_____
_____
_____
_____
_____
_____
_____
_____
_____
_____

Weekly Expense Tracker

Month :   Week Of :   Budget :

Monday   Date ..../......./.......

Description	Amount
Total	

Tuesday   Date ..../......./.......

Description	Amount
Total	

Wednesday   Date ..../......./.......

Description	Amount
Total	

Thursday   Date ..../......./.......

Description	Amount
Total	

Weekly Expense Tracker

Total Expenses :   **Balance :**

Friday   Date ..../......./.......

Description	Amount
Total	

Saturday   Date ..../......./.......

Description	Amount
Total	

Sunday   Date ..../......./.......

Description	Amount
Total	

Notes

_____

_____

_____

_____

_____

_____

_____

_____

_____

_____

Weekly Expense Tracker

Month : _____   Week Of : _____   Budget : _____

Monday   Date ..../......./.......

Description	Amount
Total	

Tuesday   Date ..../......./.......

Description	Amount
Total	

Wednesday   Date ..../......./.......

Description	Amount
Total	

Thursday   Date ..../......./.......

Description	Amount
Total	

Weekly Expense Tracker

Total Expenses :   Balance :

Friday   Date ..../......./.......

Description	Amount
Total	

Saturday   Date ..../......./.......

Description	Amount
Total	

Sunday   Date ..../......./.......

Description	Amount
Total	

Notes

Monthly Budget

Income		
Income 1		
Income 2		
Other Income		
TOTAL INCOME		

Expenses

Month :

Budget :

Bill To Be Paid	Date Due	Amount	Paid	Note
			○	
			○	
			○	
			○	
			○	
			○	
			○	
			○	
			○	
			○	
			○	
			○	
			○	
			○	
			○	
			○	
			○	
			○	
			○	
TOTAL				

Monthly Budget

Other Expenses	Date	Amount	Note
TOTAL			

TOTAL INCOME

TOTAL EXPENSES

DIFFERENCE

Notes

Weekly Expense Tracker

Month :   Week Of :   Budget :

Monday   Date ..../......./.......

Description	Amount
Total	

Tuesday   Date ..../......./.......

Description	Amount
Total	

Wednesday   Date ..../......./.......

Description	Amount
Total	

Thursday   Date ..../......./.......

Description	Amount
Total	

Weekly Expense Tracker

Total Expenses :   Balance :

Friday   Date ....../....../......

Description	Amount
Total	

Saturday   Date ....../....../......

Description	Amount
Total	

Sunday   Date ....../....../......

Description	Amount
Total	

Notes

_____
_____
_____
_____
_____
_____
_____
_____
_____

Weekly Expense Tracker

Month : _____   Week Of : _____   Budget : _____

Monday
Date ..../......./.......

Description	Amount
Total	

Tuesday
Date ..../......./.......

Description	Amount
Total	

Wednesday
Date ..../......./.......

Description	Amount
Total	

Thursday
Date ..../......./.......

Description	Amount
Total	

Weekly Expense Tracker

Total Expenses :   Balance :

Friday
Date ..../......./.......

Description	Amount
Total	

Saturday
Date ..../......./.......

Description	Amount
Total	

Sunday
Date ..../......./.......

Description	Amount
Total	

Notes

Weekly Expense Tracker

Month : _____   Week Of : _____   Budget : _____

Monday   Date ..../......./.......

Description	Amount
Total	

Tuesday   Date ..../......./.......

Description	Amount
Total	

Wednesday   Date ..../......./.......

Description	Amount
Total	

Thursday   Date ..../......./.......

Description	Amount
Total	

Weekly Expense Tracker

Total Expenses :   **Balance :**

Friday   Date ..../......./.......

Description	Amount
Total	

Saturday   Date ..../......./.......

Description	Amount
Total	

Sunday   Date ..../......./.......

Description	Amount
Total	

Notes

_____
_____
_____
_____
_____
_____
_____
_____
_____
_____

Weekly Expense Tracker

Month :   Week Of :   Budget :

Monday   Date ....../....../......

Description	Amount
Total	

Tuesday   Date ....../....../......

Description	Amount
Total	

Wednesday   Date ....../....../......

Description	Amount
Total	

Thursday   Date ....../....../......

Description	Amount
Total	

Weekly Expense Tracker

Total Expenses : _____   Balance : _____

Friday   Date ..../......./.......

Description	Amount
Total	

Saturday   Date ..../......./.......

Description	Amount
Total	

Sunday   Date ..../......./.......

Description	Amount
Total	

Notes

_____
_____
_____
_____
_____
_____
_____
_____
_____

Weekly Expense Tracker

Month :   Week Of :   Budget :

Monday   Date ..../......./.......

Description	Amount
Total	

Tuesday   Date ..../......./.......

Description	Amount
Total	

Wednesday   Date ..../......./.......

Description	Amount
Total	

Thursday   Date ..../......./.......

Description	Amount
Total	

Weekly Expense Tracker

Total Expenses :   Balance :

Friday   Date ..../......./.......

Description	Amount
Total	

Saturday   Date ..../......./.......

Description	Amount
Total	

Sunday   Date ..../......./.......

Description	Amount
Total	

Notes

_____
_____
_____
_____
_____
_____
_____
_____
_____
_____
_____

Monthly Budget

Expenses

Income		
Income 1		
Income 2		
Other Income		
TOTAL INCOME		

Month :

Budget :

Bill To Be Paid	Date Due	Amount	Paid	Note
			◯	
			◯	
			◯	
			◯	
			◯	
			◯	
			◯	
			◯	
			◯	
			◯	
			◯	
			◯	
			◯	
			◯	
			◯	
			◯	
			◯	
			◯	
			◯	
TOTAL				

Monthly Budget

Other Expenses	Date	Amount	Note
TOTAL			

TOTAL INCOME

TOTAL EXPENSES

DIFFERENCE

Notes

Weekly Expense Tracker

Month :   Week Of :   Budget :

Monday   Date ..../......./.......

Description	Amount
Total	

Tuesday   Date ..../......./.......

Description	Amount
Total	

Wednesday   Date ..../......./.......

Description	Amount
Total	

Thursday   Date ..../......./.......

Description	Amount
Total	

Weekly Expense Tracker

Total Expenses :   **Balance :**

Friday   Date ..../......./.......

Description	Amount
Total	

Saturday   Date ..../......./.......

Description	Amount
Total	

Sunday   Date ..../......./.......

Description	Amount
Total	

Notes

_____

_____

_____

_____

_____

_____

_____

_____

_____

_____

Weekly Expense Tracker

Month :   Week Of :   Budget :

Monday
Date ..../......./.......

Description	Amount
Total	

Tuesday
Date ..../......./.......

Description	Amount
Total	

Wednesday
Date ..../......./.......

Description	Amount
Total	

Thursday
Date ..../......./.......

Description	Amount
Total	

Weekly Expense Tracker

Total Expenses :   Balance :

Friday   Date ..../......./.......

Description	Amount
Total	

Saturday   Date ..../......./.......

Description	Amount
Total	

Sunday   Date ..../......./.......

Description	Amount
Total	

Notes

Weekly Expense Tracker

Month :   Week Of :   Budget :

Monday   Date ……/……/……

Description	Amount
Total	

Tuesday   Date ……/……/……

Description	Amount
Total	

Wednesday   Date ……/……/……

Description	Amount
Total	

Thursday   Date ……/……/……

Description	Amount
Total	

Weekly Expense Tracker

Total Expenses : _____   **Balance :** _____

Friday
Date ..../......./.......

Description	Amount
Total	

Saturday
Date ..../......./.......

Description	Amount
Total	

Sunday
Date ..../......./.......

Description	Amount
Total	

Notes

_____

_____

_____

_____

_____

_____

_____

_____

_____

_____

Weekly Expense Tracker

Month :   **Week Of :**   **Budget :**

Monday   Date ..../......./.......

Description	Amount
Total	

Tuesday   Date ..../......./.......

Description	Amount
Total	

Wednesday   Date ..../......./.......

Description	Amount
Total	

Thursday   Date ..../......./.......

Description	Amount
Total	

Weekly Expense Tracker

Total Expenses :   **Balance :**

Friday
Date ..../......./.......

Description	Amount
Total	

Saturday
Date ..../......./.......

Description	Amount
Total	

Sunday
Date ..../......./.......

Description	Amount
Total	

Notes

Weekly Expense Tracker

Month :   Week Of :   Budget :

Monday   Date ..../......./.......

Description	Amount
Total	

Tuesday   Date ..../......./.......

Description	Amount
Total	

Wednesday   Date ..../......./.......

Description	Amount
Total	

Thursday   Date ..../......./.......

Description	Amount
Total	

Weekly Expense Tracker

Total Expenses :   **Balance :**

Friday   Date ....../....../......

Description	Amount
Total	

Saturday   Date ....../....../......

Description	Amount
Total	

Sunday   Date ....../....../......

Description	Amount
Total	

Notes

_____
_____
_____
_____
_____
_____
_____
_____
_____
_____

Monthly Budget

Income		
Income 1		
Income 2		
Other Income		
TOTAL INCOME		

Expenses

Month :

Budget :

Bill To Be Paid	Date Due	Amount	Paid	Note
			◯	
			◯	
			◯	
			◯	
			◯	
			◯	
			◯	
			◯	
			◯	
			◯	
			◯	
			◯	
			◯	
			◯	
			◯	
			◯	
			◯	
			◯	
			◯	
			◯	
TOTAL				

Monthly Budget

Other Expenses	Date	Amount	Note
TOTAL			

TOTAL INCOME

TOTAL EXPENSES

DIFFERENCE

Notes

Weekly Expense Tracker

Month :   Week Of :   Budget :

Monday   Date ..../......./.......

Description	Amount
Total	

Tuesday   Date ..../......./.......

Description	Amount
Total	

Wednesday   Date ..../......./.......

Description	Amount
Total	

Thursday   Date ..../......./.......

Description	Amount
Total	

Weekly Expense Tracker

Total Expenses :   Balance :

Friday
Date ..../......./.......

Description	Amount
Total	

Saturday
Date ..../......./.......

Description	Amount
Total	

Sunday
Date ..../......./.......

Description	Amount
Total	

Notes

Weekly Expense Tracker

Month :   **Week Of :**   **Budget :**

Monday   Date ....../....../......

Description	Amount
Total	

Tuesday   Date ....../....../......

Description	Amount
Total	

Wednesday   Date ....../....../......

Description	Amount
Total	

Thursday   Date ....../....../......

Description	Amount
Total	

Weekly Expense Tracker

Total Expenses :   **Balance :**

Friday   Date ..../......./.......

Description	Amount
Total	

Saturday   Date ..../......./.......

Description	Amount
Total	

Sunday   Date ..../......./.......

Description	Amount
Total	

Notes

Weekly Expense Tracker

Month :   Week Of :   Budget :

Monday   Date ..../......./.......

Description	Amount
Total	

Tuesday   Date ..../......./.......

Description	Amount
Total	

Wednesday   Date ..../......./.......

Description	Amount
Total	

Thursday   Date ..../......./.......

Description	Amount
Total	

Weekly Expense Tracker

Total Expenses :   **Balance :**

Friday   Date ..../......./.......

Description	Amount
Total	

Saturday   Date ..../......./.......

Description	Amount
Total	

Sunday   Date ..../......./.......

Description	Amount
Total	

Notes

_____
_____
_____
_____
_____
_____
_____
_____
_____
_____

Weekly Expense Tracker

Month : _____   Week Of : _____   Budget : _____

Monday   Date ..../......./.......

Description	Amount
Total	

Tuesday   Date ..../......./.......

Description	Amount
Total	

Wednesday   Date ..../......./.......

Description	Amount
Total	

Thursday   Date ..../......./.......

Description	Amount
Total	

Weekly Expense Tracker

Total Expenses :   **Balance :**

Friday   Date ..../......./.......

Description	Amount
Total	

Saturday   Date ..../......./.......

Description	Amount
Total	

Sunday   Date ..../......./.......

Description	Amount
Total	

Notes

_____

_____

_____

_____

_____

_____

_____

_____

_____

Weekly Expense Tracker

Month :   Week Of :   Budget :

Monday   Date ..../......./.......

Description	Amount
Total	

Tuesday   Date ..../......./.......

Description	Amount
Total	

Wednesday   Date ..../......./.......

Description	Amount
Total	

Thursday   Date ..../......./.......

Description	Amount
Total	

Weekly Expense Tracker

Total Expenses :   **Balance :**

Friday
Date ..../......./.......

Description	Amount
Total	

Saturday
Date ..../......./.......

Description	Amount
Total	

Sunday
Date ..../......./.......

Description	Amount
Total	

Notes

_____

_____

_____

_____

_____

_____

_____

_____

_____

Monthly Budget

Income		
Income 1		
Income 2		
Other Income		
TOTAL INCOME		

Expenses

Month :

Budget :

Bill To Be Paid	Date Due	Amount	Paid	Note
			◯	
			◯	
			◯	
			◯	
			◯	
			◯	
			◯	
			◯	
			◯	
			◯	
			◯	
			◯	
			◯	
			◯	
			◯	
			◯	
			◯	
			◯	
			◯	
TOTAL				

Monthly Budget

Other Expenses	Date	Amount	Note
TOTAL			

TOTAL INCOME

TOTAL EXPENSES

DIFFERENCE

Notes

Weekly Expense Tracker

Month :   Week Of :   Budget :

Monday
Date ..../......./.......

Description	Amount
Total	

Tuesday
Date ..../......./.......

Description	Amount
Total	

Wednesday
Date ..../......./.......

Description	Amount
Total	

Thursday
Date ..../......./.......

Description	Amount
Total	

Weekly Expense Tracker

Total Expenses :   **Balance :**

Friday   Date ..../......./.......

Description	Amount
Total	

Saturday   Date ..../......./.......

Description	Amount
Total	

Sunday   Date ..../......./.......

Description	Amount
Total	

Notes

Weekly Expense Tracker

Month :   **Week Of :**   **Budget :**

Monday   Date ..../......./.......

Description	Amount
Total	

Tuesday   Date ..../......./.......

Description	Amount
Total	

Wednesday   Date ..../......./.......

Description	Amount
Total	

Thursday   Date ..../......./.......

Description	Amount
Total	

Weekly Expense Tracker

Total Expenses :   **Balance :**

Friday   Date ..../......./.......

Description	Amount
Total	

Saturday   Date ..../......./.......

Description	Amount
Total	

Sunday   Date ..../......./.......

Description	Amount
Total	

Notes

Weekly Expense Tracker

Month : ....   Week Of : ....   Budget : ....

Monday   Date ..../......./.......

Description	Amount
Total	

Tuesday   Date ..../......./.......

Description	Amount
Total	

Wednesday   Date ..../......./.......

Description	Amount
Total	

Thursday   Date ..../......./.......

Description	Amount
Total	

Weekly Expense Tracker

Total Expenses :   **Balance :**

Friday   Date ..../........./........

Description	Amount
Total	

Saturday   Date ..../........./........

Description	Amount
Total	

Sunday   Date ..../........./........

Description	Amount
Total	

Notes

_____
_____
_____
_____
_____
_____
_____
_____
_____
_____

Weekly Expense Tracker

Month :   Week Of :   Budget :

Monday   Date ..../......./.......

Description	Amount
Total	

Tuesday   Date ..../......./.......

Description	Amount
Total	

Wednesday   Date ..../......./.......

Description	Amount
Total	

Thursday   Date ..../......./.......

Description	Amount
Total	

Weekly Expense Tracker

Total Expenses :   **Balance :**

Friday   Date ..../......./.......

Description	Amount
Total	

Saturday   Date ..../......./.......

Description	Amount
Total	

Sunday   Date ..../......./.......

Description	Amount
Total	

Notes

_____

_____

_____

_____

_____

_____

_____

_____

_____

_____

Weekly Expense Tracker

Month :   Week Of :   Budget :

Monday   Date ..../......./.......

Description	Amount
Total	

Tuesday   Date ..../......./.......

Description	Amount
Total	

Wednesday   Date ..../......./.......

Description	Amount
Total	

Thursday   Date ..../......./.......

Description	Amount
Total	

Weekly Expense Tracker

Total Expenses :   Balance :

Friday   Date ..../......./.......

Description	Amount
Total	

Saturday   Date ..../......./.......

Description	Amount
Total	

Sunday   Date ..../......./.......

Description	Amount
Total	

Notes

_____
_____
_____
_____
_____
_____
_____
_____
_____

Monthly Budget

Expenses

Income		
Income 1		
Income 2		
Other Income		
TOTAL INCOME		

Month :

Budget :

Bill To Be Paid	Date Due	Amount	Paid	Note
			○	
			○	
			○	
			○	
			○	
			○	
			○	
			○	
			○	
			○	
			○	
			○	
			○	
			○	
			○	
			○	
			○	
			○	
TOTAL				

Monthly Budget

Other Expenses	Date	Amount	Note
TOTAL			

TOTAL INCOME

TOTAL EXPENSES

DIFFERENCE

Notes

Weekly Expense Tracker

Month :   Week Of :   Budget :

Monday   Date ..../......./.......

Description	Amount
Total	

Tuesday   Date ..../......./.......

Description	Amount
Total	

Wednesday   Date ..../......./.......

Description	Amount
Total	

Thursday   Date ..../......./.......

Description	Amount
Total	

Weekly Expense Tracker

Total Expenses :   **Balance :**

Friday   Date ..../......./.......

Description	Amount
Total	

Saturday   Date ..../......./.......

Description	Amount
Total	

Sunday   Date ..../......./.......

Description	Amount
Total	

Notes

Weekly Expense Tracker

Month :   Week Of :   Budget :

Monday   Date ....../....../......

Description	Amount
Total	

Tuesday   Date ....../....../......

Description	Amount
Total	

Wednesday   Date ....../....../......

Description	Amount
Total	

Thursday   Date ....../....../......

Description	Amount
Total	

Weekly Expense Tracker

Total Expenses :　　　　　　　　　　　　　　**Balance :**

Friday　　　Date ..../......./.......

Description	Amount
Total	

Saturday　　　Date ..../......./.......

Description	Amount
Total	

Sunday　　　Date ..../......./.......

Description	Amount
Total	

Notes

Weekly Expense Tracker

Month :   Week Of :   Budget :

Monday   Date ..../......./.......

Description	Amount
Total	

Tuesday   Date ..../......./.......

Description	Amount
Total	

Wednesday   Date ..../......./.......

Description	Amount
Total	

Thursday   Date ..../......./.......

Description	Amount
Total	

Weekly Expense Tracker

Total Expenses :   **Balance :**

Friday   Date ..../......./.......

Description	Amount
Total	

Saturday   Date ..../......./.......

Description	Amount
Total	

Sunday   Date ..../......./.......

Description	Amount
Total	

Notes

Weekly Expense Tracker

Month :   **Week Of :**   **Budget :**

Monday   Date ..../......./.......

Description	Amount
Total	

Tuesday   Date ..../......./.......

Description	Amount
Total	

Wednesday   Date ..../......./.......

Description	Amount
Total	

Thursday   Date ..../......./.......

Description	Amount
Total	

Weekly Expense Tracker

Total Expenses :   Balance :

Friday   Date ..../......./.......

Description	Amount
Total	

Saturday   Date ..../......./.......

Description	Amount
Total	

Sunday   Date ..../......./.......

Description	Amount
Total	

Notes

Weekly Expense Tracker

Month : _____   Week Of : _____   Budget : _____

Monday   Date ..../......./.......

Description	Amount
Total	

Tuesday   Date ..../......./.......

Description	Amount
Total	

Wednesday   Date ..../......./.......

Description	Amount
Total	

Thursday   Date ..../......./.......

Description	Amount
Total	

Weekly Expense Tracker

Total Expenses :   **Balance :**

Friday
Date ….…/….…/….…

Description	Amount
Total	

Saturday
Date ….…/….…/….…

Description	Amount
Total	

Sunday
Date ….…/….…/….…

Description	Amount
Total	

Notes

Monthly Budget

Income		
Income 1		
Income 2		
Other Income		
TOTAL INCOME		

Expenses

Month :

Budget :

Bill To Be Paid	Date Due	Amount	Paid	Note
			○	
			○	
			○	
			○	
			○	
			○	
			○	
			○	
			○	
			○	
			○	
			○	
			○	
			○	
			○	
			○	
			○	
			○	
			○	
TOTAL				

Monthly Budget

Other Expenses	Date	Amount	Note
TOTAL			

TOTAL INCOME

TOTAL EXPENSES

DIFFERENCE

Notes

Weekly Expense Tracker

Month :   Week Of :   Budget :

Monday   Date ..../......./.......

Description	Amount
Total	

Tuesday   Date ..../......./.......

Description	Amount
Total	

Wednesday   Date ..../......./.......

Description	Amount
Total	

Thursday   Date ..../......./.......

Description	Amount
Total	

Weekly Expense Tracker

Total Expenses :   **Balance :**

Friday   Date ..../......./.......

Description	Amount
Total	

Saturday   Date ..../......./.......

Description	Amount
Total	

Sunday   Date ..../......./.......

Description	Amount
Total	

Notes

Weekly Expense Tracker

Month : ....   Week Of : ....   Budget : ....

Monday   Date ..../......./.......

Description	Amount
Total	

Tuesday   Date ..../......./.......

Description	Amount
Total	

Wednesday   Date ..../......./.......

Description	Amount
Total	

Thursday   Date ..../......./.......

Description	Amount
Total	

Weekly Expense Tracker

Total Expenses :   **Balance :**

Friday   Date ..../......./.......

Description	Amount
Total	

Saturday   Date ..../......./.......

Description	Amount
Total	

Sunday   Date ..../......./.......

Description	Amount
Total	

Notes

Weekly Expense Tracker

Month : _____   Week Of : _____   Budget : _____

Monday
Date ..../......./.......

Description	Amount
Total	

Tuesday
Date ..../......./.......

Description	Amount
Total	

Wednesday
Date ..../......./.......

Description	Amount
Total	

Thursday
Date ..../......./.......

Description	Amount
Total	

Weekly Expense Tracker

Total Expenses :   **Balance :**

Friday   Date …..../…...../…......

Description	Amount
Total	

Saturday   Date …..../…...../…......

Description	Amount
Total	

Sunday   Date …..../…...../…......

Description	Amount
Total	

Notes

Weekly Expense Tracker

Month :   Week Of :   Budget :

Monday   Date ..../......./.......

Description	Amount
Total	

Tuesday   Date ..../......./.......

Description	Amount
Total	

Wednesday   Date ..../......./.......

Description	Amount
Total	

Thursday   Date ..../......./.......

Description	Amount
Total	

Weekly Expense Tracker

Total Expenses : _____   Balance : _____

Friday   Date ..../......./.......

Description	Amount
Total	

Saturday   Date ..../......./.......

Description	Amount
Total	

Sunday   Date ..../......./.......

Description	Amount
Total	

Notes

_____
_____
_____
_____
_____
_____
_____
_____
_____

Weekly Expense Tracker

Month :   Week Of :   Budget :

Monday   Date ..../......./.......

Description	Amount
Total	

Tuesday   Date ..../......./.......

Description	Amount
Total	

Wednesday   Date ..../......./.......

Description	Amount
Total	

Thursday   Date ..../......./.......

Description	Amount
Total	

Weekly Expense Tracker

Total Expenses :   Balance :

Friday

Date ….../….../…....

Description	Amount
Total	

Saturday

Date ….../….../…....

Description	Amount
Total	

Sunday

Date ….../….../…....

Description	Amount
Total	

Notes

_____

_____

_____

_____

_____

_____

_____

_____

Monthly Budget

Income		
Income 1		
Income 2		
Other Income		
TOTAL INCOME		

Expenses

Month :

Budget :

Bill To Be Paid	Date Due	Amount	Paid	Note
			○	
			○	
			○	
			○	
			○	
			○	
			○	
			○	
			○	
			○	
			○	
			○	
			○	
			○	
			○	
			○	
			○	
			○	
			○	
TOTAL				

Monthly Budget

Other Expenses	Date	Amount	Note
TOTAL			

TOTAL INCOME

TOTAL EXPENSES

DIFFERENCE

Notes

Weekly Expense Tracker

Month :   Week Of :   Budget :

Monday Date ..../......./.......

Description	Amount
Total	

Tuesday Date ..../......./.......

Description	Amount
Total	

Wednesday Date ..../......./.......

Description	Amount
Total	

Thursday Date ..../......./.......

Description	Amount
Total	

Weekly Expense Tracker

Total Expenses :   **Balance :**

Friday   Date ..../......./.......

Description	Amount
Total	

Saturday   Date ..../......./.......

Description	Amount
Total	

Sunday   Date ..../......./.......

Description	Amount
Total	

Notes

_____
_____
_____
_____
_____
_____
_____
_____
_____

Weekly Expense Tracker

Month : _____   Week Of : _____   Budget : _____

Monday   Date ..../......./.......

Description	Amount
Total	

Tuesday   Date ..../......./.......

Description	Amount
Total	

Wednesday   Date ..../......./.......

Description	Amount
Total	

Thursday   Date ..../......./.......

Description	Amount
Total	

Weekly Expense Tracker

Total Expenses :   Balance :

Friday   Date ..../......./.......

Description	Amount
Total	

Saturday   Date ..../......./.......

Description	Amount
Total	

Sunday   Date ..../......./.......

Description	Amount
Total	

Notes

Weekly Expense Tracker

Month :   Week Of :   Budget :

Monday   Date ..../......./.......

Description	Amount
Total	

Tuesday   Date ..../......./.......

Description	Amount
Total	

Wednesday   Date ..../......./.......

Description	Amount
Total	

Thursday   Date ..../......./.......

Description	Amount
Total	

Weekly Expense Tracker

Total Expenses :

Balance :

Friday

Date ..../......./.......

Description	Amount
Total	

Saturday

Date ..../......./.......

Description	Amount
Total	

Sunday

Date ..../......./.......

Description	Amount
Total	

Notes

_____

_____

_____

_____

_____

_____

_____

_____

_____

_____

Weekly Expense Tracker

Month :   Week Of :   Budget :

Monday   Date ..../......./.......

Description	Amount
Total	

Tuesday   Date ..../......./.......

Description	Amount
Total	

Wednesday   Date ..../......./.......

Description	Amount
Total	

Thursday   Date ..../......./.......

Description	Amount
Total	

Weekly Expense Tracker

Total Expenses :   **Balance :**

Friday   Date ..../......./.......

Description	Amount
Total	

Saturday   Date ..../......./.......

Description	Amount
Total	

Sunday   Date ..../......./.......

Description	Amount
Total	

Notes

Weekly Expense Tracker

Month :   Week Of :   Budget :

Monday   Date ….../….../…...

Description	Amount
Total	

Tuesday   Date ….../….../…...

Description	Amount
Total	

Wednesday   Date ….../….../…...

Description	Amount
Total	

Thursday   Date ….../….../…...

Description	Amount
Total	

Weekly Expense Tracker

Total Expenses :   **Balance :**

Friday   Date ....../....../......

Description	Amount
Total	

Saturday   Date ....../....../......

Description	Amount
Total	

Sunday   Date ....../....../......

Description	Amount
Total	

Notes

_____
_____
_____
_____
_____
_____
_____
_____
_____

Monthly Budget

Income		
Income 1		
Income 2		
Other Income		
TOTAL INCOME		

Expenses

Month :

Budget :

Bill To Be Paid	Date Due	Amount	Paid	Note
			◯	
			◯	
			◯	
			◯	
			◯	
			◯	
			◯	
			◯	
			◯	
			◯	
			◯	
			◯	
			◯	
			◯	
			◯	
			◯	
			◯	
			◯	
			◯	
			◯	
TOTAL				

Monthly Budget

Other Expenses	Date	Amount	Note
TOTAL			

TOTAL INCOME

TOTAL EXPENSES

DIFFERENCE

Notes
_____
_____
_____
_____
_____

Weekly Expense Tracker

Month :   Week Of :   Budget :

Monday   Date ..../......./.......

Description	Amount
Total	

Tuesday   Date ..../......./.......

Description	Amount
Total	

Wednesday   Date ..../......./.......

Description	Amount
Total	

Thursday   Date ..../......./.......

Description	Amount
Total	

Weekly Expense Tracker

Total Expenses :   Balance :

Friday   Date ….…./….…./….…

Description	Amount
Total	

Saturday   Date ….…./….…./….…

Description	Amount
Total	

Sunday   Date ….…./….…./….…

Description	Amount
Total	

Notes

_____
_____
_____
_____
_____
_____
_____
_____
_____
_____
_____

Weekly Expense Tracker

Month :   Week Of :   Budget :

Monday   Date ....../....../......

Description	Amount
Total	

Tuesday   Date ....../....../......

Description	Amount
Total	

Wednesday   Date ....../....../......

Description	Amount
Total	

Thursday   Date ....../....../......

Description	Amount
Total	

Weekly Expense Tracker

Total Expenses :   **Balance :**

Friday
Date ..../......./.......

Description	Amount
Total	

Saturday
Date ..../......./.......

Description	Amount
Total	

Sunday
Date ..../......./.......

Description	Amount
Total	

Notes

_____
_____
_____
_____
_____
_____
_____
_____
_____
_____

Weekly Expense Tracker

Month :　　　　　　　**Week Of :**　　　　　　　**Budget :**

Monday　　Date …..../…..../…....

Description	Amount
Total	

Tuesday　　Date …..../…..../…....

Description	Amount
Total	

Wednesday　　Date …..../…..../…....

Description	Amount
Total	

Thursday　　Date …..../…..../…....

Description	Amount
Total	

Weekly Expense Tracker

Total Expenses :   **Balance :**

Friday   Date ..../......./.......

Description	Amount
Total	

Saturday   Date ..../......./.......

Description	Amount
Total	

Sunday   Date ..../......./.......

Description	Amount
Total	

Notes

_____

_____

_____

_____

_____

_____

_____

_____

Weekly Expense Tracker

Month :   Week Of :   Budget :

Monday   Date ..../......./......

Description	Amount
Total	

Tuesday   Date ..../......./......

Description	Amount
Total	

Wednesday   Date ..../......./......

Description	Amount
Total	

Thursday   Date ..../......./......

Description	Amount
Total	

Weekly Expense Tracker

Total Expenses :   Balance :

Friday
Date ..../......./.......

Description	Amount
Total	

Saturday
Date ..../......./.......

Description	Amount
Total	

Sunday
Date ..../......./.......

Description	Amount
Total	

Notes

_____
_____
_____
_____
_____
_____
_____
_____
_____
_____

Weekly Expense Tracker

Month : _____   Week Of : _____   Budget : _____

Monday   Date ..../......./.......

Description	Amount
Total	

Tuesday   Date ..../......./.......

Description	Amount
Total	

Wednesday   Date ..../......./.......

Description	Amount
Total	

Thursday   Date ..../......./.......

Description	Amount
Total	

Weekly Expense Tracker

Total Expenses :   **Balance :**

Friday   Date ..../......./.......

Description	Amount
Total	

Saturday   Date ..../......./.......

Description	Amount
Total	

Sunday   Date ..../......./.......

Description	Amount
Total	

Notes

_____
_____
_____
_____
_____
_____
_____
_____
_____

Notes